W9-ARQ-217

Comments from people who attended Jenifer O'Leary's workshops on curriculum planning:

"Enjoyable, helpful in reinforcing non-guilt about not using formal curriculum."

———————

"Lots of good ideas and a calm, realistic approach."

———————

"Very informative. Excellent. I ...."

WRITE YOUR OWN CURRICULUM

CURRICULUM

A Complete Guide to Planning,

Organizing and Documenting

Homeschool Curriculums

WRITE YOUR OWN CURRICULUM

A Complete Guide to Planning,

Organizing and Documenting

Homeschool Curriculums

Jenifer O'Leary

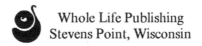 Whole Life Publishing
Stevens Point, Wisconsin

First Edition

Library of Congress Catalog Number 93-60801

ISBN 1-883947-24-3

Cover Design By Jenifer O'Leary

PUBLISHED BY
Whole Life Publishing Co.
P.O. Box 936
Stevens Point, WI 54481-0936

Dedicated to homeschoolers everywhere

ABOUT THE ARTIST
Wonderfully sensitive, witty and fun, Zac Baldus is an inspired and talented young artist. Rarely does one find Zac without his sketchbook nearby. His unique personal style is the result of many years of working independently and with a variety of art teachers.

Acknowledgements

I wish to extend my gratitude to all the generous people who supported me in this endeavor. To those who so willingly read the manuscript and sent their comments and feedback. To my homeschooling comrades who, over the years, have spent so many hours discussing with me how children learn and the pros and cons of structure. To the many eager participants in my sessions at the Wisconsin Homeschoolers Conference who shared with me many of their experiences, needs, concerns and methods.

Thank you Jim, my best friend, husband and father of my sons, for providing me with the financial and emotional support I needed to continue homeschooling, for helping me up when I'd fall and for an undying faith and commitment to the whole process... Thank you, I love you.

Thank you Kyle and Sean for being two of the best teachers I'll ever come across, from whom I've learned so much about love, life and learning. It has been an honor and a privilege parenting both of you. I love you.

Thank you Shirley Ebel (mom) for opening your office to me, teaching me all about your computer, and for believing in me. I love you.

Thanks Gael Stepanek for teaching me to take risks, extend my peripheral boundaries, develop a clear focus and commit to it completely and for helping me discover my need for more structure. I love you.

Special thanks go to Joe and Maureen Ebel for so graciously offering your time, services and support to get this project off the ground. Your time and energies are appreciated more than you'll ever realize.

Thanks Mary Licari, my partner in crime, for loving, supporting and helping me, and for co/mothering my boys when they (or I) needed it.

Table of Contents

PART 3

Additional Helps

INTRODUCTION

A lot has been written about child-led learning and its superiority over our modern approach to education. In child-led learning, the child learns naturally from life, at his or her own pace, without the distraction of being graded and labeled. Everything is connected. Subjects are found relevant, in their natural context, not separated into little boxes and classes, isolated and meaningless.

As homeschool parents it is our job to inspire, encourage and guide our children through the maze of available information and knowledge, down the path they are most inclined to follow. We need to provide them with a broad range of experiences. It is our job to allow them the space and time they require to formulate intelligent questions, introduce them to the resources available and show them how to find the answers they need. We need to encourage seeking and learning instead of knowing and having.

When we first started homeschooling and our boys were in the earliest grades, everyday was spontaneous. We moved freely from one thing to the next and did most things together. As they grew into the middle grades, our diverse interests often pulled us in different directions. Old enough at the time to be more independent in their studies, I found that they didn't want to be left on their own but looked to us for guidance and direction in education the same as they did in so many other aspects of their growth. They wanted plenty of encouragement. They wanted us to show an interest in their educational development, to help them identify their strengths and weaknesses, to help them find their way over the challenging hurdles they came upon. They wanted to know what their options were as to the best approach to a problem or subject area.

We began adding more structure to our program. We experimented with goal setting, project planning and scheduling. We explored several possibilities for record keeping and organization. Recognizing and honoring our constantly changing interests and needs was an important part of the process for us, requiring patience and flexibility.

This book was created to help you in designing your own personalized curriculums; how to start, what to study and ways to organize and document it all. It demonstrates what approaches worked for us and how we changed our format over the years, to fit our lifestyle and educational needs.

PART ONE

Custom Tailored Curriculums

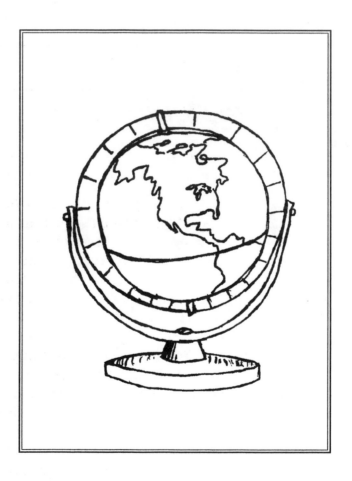

CHAPTER 1

Magic Formulas

Some people seem to feel that there are certain magic formulas to which we must adhere in order to correctly and completely educate our children. Such attitudes only serve to intimidate us. The fact is, there is no such formula. How can there be, in a world that is constantly changing? How can we be sure of what challenges our children will face in their future? Schools don't have such a formula, otherwise they wouldn't be changing their curriculums so often. Besides, if we had that much faith in the way schools educate, many of us wouldn't be homeschooling. Keep in mind that school curriculum directors, in setting up their curriculums, are counting hours. They must occupy classrooms full of children all day for a mandated number of days. Typically curriculums are planned by strangers, people from textbook companies who have never met the students for whom they are planning and have no idea of their individual interests or needs. This results in teaching inefficiencies such as lack of spontaneity and not teaching "from the heart" or "to the moment."

You may be concerned that writing your own plan will take too much time. The time you spend in planning a curriculum tailored to suit the needs and interests of your family will be better spent than the time it takes to convince your children to stick with a dry, boring, generic curriculum that they're not even interested in. The beauty of self-directed learning is teaching in the moment; teaching one on one high interest-level activities; being able to change plans and be spontaneous; and being freed to indulge, expand on or drop a subject as you see fit. You will not have to pressure or bribe your students if the material is vital to them. You will only need to support and encourage them to grow. Homeschooling is learning together - learning from life itself. It is not easier or safer to buy a curriculum and it certainly isn't cheaper. When it comes to purchasing materials you can spend as much or as little money as you want. You can educate your children completely with no financial investment at all. The only pressures or deadlines you have will be the ones you set yourself.

Another common concern people have when considering curriculum planning is evaluations. How will you know how your child is doing? Ask yourself these questions: Is your child secure? Does she seem to get along O.K.? Can she answer to the demands and challenges put to her by peers and society? It doesn't take special tests to see how your child is getting along. Working one on one puts you in a situation where it is easy to see whether or not she understands the material. When she doesn't, you just spend a little more time with her.

There are many facets of education that are impossible to evaluate, judge or measure with tests. Rest assured, if you are doing interesting things, enjoying each other and learning how and where to find answers, you're probably doing fine. World Book has a pamphlet available titled *Typical Course of Study K-12* (see appendix). If you look through it, you'll find that many subjects and topics are repeated every other year. Each time, I'm sure the focus would be in greater depth and at an advanced level. This does not have to happen in your homeschool unless you want it to. Chances are when the student is ready, the material will be absorbed more completely, all at once, eliminating the need for so much repetition and review. You know how it is when you're really interested in what you're doing... you can't get enough of it. You want to totally saturate yourself in information and experiences. That kind of learning has real staying power. Generally speaking, the child is most absorbed in an activity he is learning the most from.

If you still feel the need or desire to test, tests are available through your local school district, private schools, or through mail order. (Check some of the catalogs listed in the appendix.) Be aware that schools build their curriculums around the tests they use. Tests come with most math books and spelling tests can be made as you go. There are also quite a few workbooks available to help prepare your child for SATs and ACT's. Tests can be fun. My boys enjoy being tested. It can provide a healthy challenge and is good practice for test taking in the future. Be sure you keep a healthy attitude in this process and keep things in perspective. A student can become discouraged or encouraged depending on your reaction to the results. Be sensitive.

CHAPTER 2

Getting Started

The easiest way to start planning a curriculum is by observing. Get a notebook and keep it with you as you go about your daily tasks. Keep a watchful eye on your students and how they choose to spend their time, their reactions to people and events they experience and their interests and activities. This is best done during summer when there's less outside pressure to involve them in academics and more time for them to discover their passions, to daydream and engage in quiet contemplation and simple pleasures. I have also used this exercise mid year to tune in better and keep a good perspective on how we are doing. It helps prevent focusing too much on your desires and goals for them, at the expense of their own special interests and personal goals. Take at least a week to do this. It's fun, interesting and revealing. Becoming aware of the fact that we don't all assimilate information the same way can open the door for a much wider variety of learning possibilities. Two good books on how children learn are *Growing Up Learning*, (put out by Highlights magazine), and *In Their Own Way*, by Thomas Armstrong.The information gathered will be helpful to you in planning your curriculum and gaining an awareness of your child's strengths, weaknesses and preferred learning methods.

It may be helpful to consider what "compartments" some of these activities fit into. I suggest this because it is the way most of us have been trained to think. It is easier to deal with critics, skeptics and authorities if you learn to think in commonly accepted terms. This in no way needs to interfere with the natural flow of self-directed learning, but it will help you keep records and fulfill legal obligations as well as pave the road for possible school/college entrance in the future.

With practice you will become creative at this. Cooking becomes home-economics or culinary arts. Target practice with BB guns is marksmanship. Building a fort is construction, carpentry or engineering. Biking, skating, skiing, swimming, running and sports are all physical fitness, health or phy-ed, while boating, canoeing, camping and exploring can be titled nature studies or environmental science. Even household chores and keeping one's room clean will seem more significant when given an appropriate title: personal management, family living or domestic engineering.

Many people believe an activity has educational merit if it is assigned, but not if it is self-motivated. I believe the opposite is true. The most meaningful and useful education is self directed. In self-directed learning you will find that subjects overlap, spilling into each other until there is only one subject left...LIFE!!! That's the way it is when the world is your classroom.

Here are a few ideas for categories to use. Can you think of any activities to fit them?

> Agricultural Studies-gardening, farming, animal
>   husbandry
> Auto Maintenance
> Child Care/Child Development
> Creative Expression-art, music, dance, drama
> Role Playing

Reading - oral/silent
Listening
Comprehension
Socialization Skills
Field Trips
Religious Studies/Spiritual Development
Physics
Geometry
Sociology
Science
Language Arts
Math
Health
Computer Literacy
Business Education
Shop
Foreign Language
Philosophy
Psychiatry
Psychology

WHAT COUNTS? Wisconsin state laws require 375 hours of instruction in a progressive curriculum each year. Rather than trying to keep track of each 15 minute segment of each day (it's enough to drive you nuts!) we modeled our record keeping after school and just figured approximately how long a "school" day is for us. It's just as impossible for us to count the hours actually spent learning each day as it is for schools. Just because a student is present doesn't mean that student is receiving instruction. When I'm encouraging my boys to become well rounded academically and find educationally stimulating activities to engage in, they don't always understand what it is I'm asking for. They want to know what "counts." Anything counts as long as we can agree that it is of educational value. Caring for the sick and community service definitely count as part of our curriculum. My boys have taken credit for working on the snowmobile, a project with built in incentives. The snowmobile was an old one donated for the cause, and in the process of trying to get it running, a great deal was learned. (I am sure there is some value in Nintendo but I refuse to count it.) My boys and I have had some interesting discussions and arguments about what constitutes worthwhile and educational activities (an exercise in critical thinking in and of itself). Keep an open mind; most of us have been systemized. Again, AN ACTIVITY DOESN'T HAVE TO BE ASSIGNED OR UNPLEASANT TO HAVE MERIT.

CHAPTER 3

Deciding What To Study

It's a good idea to begin planning in spring for the next year. That gives you all summer to gather your materials. You don't have to think in terms of a school year of course. We do because that's the way it is in our community - it's the way people think and my children like it better that way. They like to start fresh in fall with new ideas and materials. They don't realize the continuum of their education; they aren't entirely aware of how much work they're actually doing in the summer. I am and I keep track of it in a notebook - labeling the various activities into their respective categories or more often than not just keeping a journal of interesting or special activities they engage in.

It feels good to really dive in when fall arrives and everyone marches off to school. We like to plan a "celebrate homeschooling" activity each fall - a picnic or canoe trip or other outing - preferably something in the great outdoors! This year our support group is planning a celebration together. We're going to the waterslide park. The weather is usually HOT and because school is back in session there are

NO LINES. What a fun way to celebrate our educational freedom!

There are many different ways to go about planning your curriculum. Try several approaches or change each year to see what works best for you. You can build the entire plan around a single important event, an interest/hobby, good books/literature or even a calendar or almanac, using the dates of certain historical events or birthdays of famous people to determine what you'll do and when. You may decide to loosely outline your plans for the year and not go into too much detail in order to be open to spontaneity. You never know what might spark an interest from your curriculum plan or where it might lead. You may initially build it around 4H, Scouts or magazines and end up scrapping the whole thing in pursuit of some wild new passion. Remain open to the moment. However, a certain amount of order and planning can be helpful, so let's begin by finding those starting points - those potential sparks of interest.

First check your legal obligations. List these off to the side somewhere for future reference. Chances are they will be filled in effortlessly as you go. Decide what it is you would like to learn/study this year. If you are concerned about what the "other" children are learning you might want to consult World Book's *Typical Course of Study K-12* (see appendix). This will give you a general idea of what is being covered and when. How you choose to go about learning any particular subject is up to you. The depth you go into, what materials you use, the approach you take and the amount of time you spend on anything will be determined by you, the students, the available materials and resources, interest levels, etc. It is not without reservation that I recommend the use of the World Book pamphlet so here's a word of warning: don't get caught up in it. You do not have to accomplish all of it. Just use it as a general guide or as a starting place to touch on subjects or ideas until you spark a stronger interest in something and go into greater depth there. Use it, but don't over use it.

Another place to look for ideas on what to study, and this one comes with the same warnings, is your local schools. Call the superintendent or curriculum coordinator at school and ask to see the curriculum that they are presently using. This can be especially helpful if you are homeschooling temporarily or plan on possibly reentering your children into school. In order to take full advantage of the alternative nature of homeschooling though, it is recommended that you use these curriculums only as a reference tool. In schools, much of the information is obtained through the use of textbooks. Generally speaking, we find textbooks to be dry and lifeless and tend to avoid them, though we have found a few to be useful at times. For instance, we use *Saxon Math* because we feel it's thorough and easy to follow. It seems to be written to the student - it's "user friendly." If your curriculum seems to be lacking in a certain subject area (due, perhaps, to the fact that your interests aren't strong there) yet you'd like to keep it well rounded, you may then choose to use a textbook and have the students work their way through it at whatever pace they set. Often this can be completed in a surprisingly short time, leaving them free for more exciting pursuits. Sometimes this can open a door to a new direction in a subject. You can find a new starting point in a textbook.

My favorite way to find ideas on what to study is to go directly to the students. Ask your students what they'd like to learn. Get everyone together and brainstorm for ideas. This is fun and often full of surprises. It fosters a sense of personal power and responsibility in the students . Keep a separate list for each student and don't forget yourself. I always write myself into the curriculum. It provides a good example, prevents burnout and it's fun. There is so much to learn in such a short lifetime. Think about it awhile. You will certainly come up with more than you can handle in a year. Don't let it overwhelm you; prioritize. If you can't come up with enough ideas, browse the library, the bookstore or any of the hundreds of catalogs available.

MORE PLACES TO GET IDEAS (free !)

Chambers of Commerce
Churches
Consumer Information Catalog (see appendix)
Companies
County Extension Agents
Factories
Friends
Government Agencies
Historical Societies
Hobbyists
Local Businesses
Field trips
Interviews
Work study
Volunteer work
Museums
Organizations
4H
Scouts
Charities
Special Interest Groups
Professionals
Public Television and Radio
Teachers
Travel Agencies
Universities
Zoos

A FEW POSSIBILITIES FROM THE LIBRARY

Almanacs
Art Atlases
Bibles
Bibliographies
Book Reviews
Books of Proverbs
Books on Tape
Business Books
Career Information
City Directories
College Guides
Computers
Dictionaries
Encyclopedias
Art
Sports
Foreign Language Dictionaries
History Books
Large Print Books
Law Books
Literary Criticism
Local Information
Magazines
Maps
Medical Manuals
Microfilm
Movies
Music
Newspapers

Pictures/Paintings
Textbooks
Thomas Register
Typewriters
Unit Kits
Videos
Young Adult Section

Some things you'll want to do all together. For example, if you start the delightful, enriching habit of evening read alouds, chances are everyone will be involved. Perhaps you can take turns reading. Creative writing is another subject that can be done as a family. Everyone can write on the same topic, each at his/her own level of understanding and expertise, or choose different topics and help each other edit. Current events and educational programs can be watched together. Seasonal topics such as Black History month (February) or Women's History month (March) can be done together. Each person perceives and responds at his/her own level of ability and understanding. Often one person's enthusiasm and interest rubs off on others. When I decided to learn to type, suddenly everyone was at the typewriter. If one person learns French, the rest are bound to pick up a bit of it. My interest and absorption in becoming familiar with birds and their songs resulted in everyone getting into it to some degree. Sometimes a topic that the students choose to study turns out to be of great interest to the parents as well. My boys wanted to learn about Native Americans, which they did. I became interested and delved into it much deeper than I ever thought I would. It is now an ongoing study that's taken me in more directions than you can imagine.

CHAPTER 4

Dynamics

When you have a list of interesting subjects for the family to investigate, organize the information into two categories, family studies and individual studies (list each student separately). If there is a large gap in the ages of your students, subjects such as math and reading/language arts are often done individually. Sometimes two students will decide to pair up on a topic of mutual interest. Some subjects lend themselves naturally to the unit study approach. Current events and calendar curriculums offer ongoing opportunities for family projects and discussions.

Unit Study

Unit study is a way to really delve into a topic of interest by gearing your entire curriculum around it. An obvious choice for this is whatever topic your children are currently most enthusiastic about. Studying different countries works especially well for unit study. You can start anywhere and branch out. The basic formula is to list all of the subject areas you want included. Then choose your topic and fill in the blanks. Your list of possible subjects may look something like this:

    Art
      Performing Arts
      Fine Arts
    Cooking
    Clothing
    Housing
    Literature and Poetry
    Creative Writing
    Science
      Inventions
      Nature
      Popular Beliefs
      Discoveries
    Religion
    Foreign Language
    Typing
    Field Trips
    History
    Architecture
    Climate
    Customs
    Currency
    Math

For instance, planning a simple garden may take you in several directions; you might start out with a seed catalog (reading, math) and end up learning about welding, to make your own tools. Or you might get into soil composition (science),and learn to compost and raise earth worms - information which you, in turn, might share with your community at a recycling seminar (speech). It might lead you into hybrids and developing your own varieties of plants (biology), or learning about heirloom/open pollinated varieties and saving your own seed from year to year. You might learn to grow your own grains and bake bread in an outdoor fire-heated oven that you made (math, science, building, cooking). You might read biographies about Luther Burbank, Thomas Jefferson or other pioneers in gardening (history).

Here is another example using oceans as the starting point. Perhaps you begin by finding biographies or autobiographies of early explorers. This might lead to reading fiction and non fiction books about sailors, pirates, coastal towns and life at sea. Then you might look into the study of some of the ocean's natural inhabitants from the largest whales to the tiniest plankton. Visit Sea World or the aquarium section of your nearest zoo or start an aquarium of your own. If your interest is strong in literature or folklore, you might want to spend some time on mythical creatures of the sea or create a collection of legends and folklore about the mysteries of the ocean from various locations around the world. You can seek out art, music, dance, drama or poetry with oceans as the subject. Create your own art inspired by your ocean studies. What can you discover about the food people get from the ocean? What can be done with seafood in

its many varied forms including vegetation? Investigate culinary customs and preferences of people on islands or in
coastal towns in different areas of the world. You may decide
to focus your studies on ships of long ago. What kind of
clothing was worn aboard ships? *Dover Publications* has a
great little coloring book about pirates and buccaneers showing different costumes and telling something about each.
Compare ships of today with those of long ago: comforts,
entertainment, food and clothes. Possible field trips may include snorkeling, scuba diving, beach combing or visiting
museums or boat builders. Enjoy videos of classic movies or
documentaries about coastal towns. Build your own boat,
either a model or the real thing.

It would be entirely possible to gear your complete
curriculum on world studies for all your homeschooling years.
Just work your way around the world choosing a country and
learning about its history, literature, people, customs, curren-
cy and language. If there is an event coming up that you want
to plan for, why not create a unit study around that? A 4H
fair or speaking contest, a camping or canoe trip, or a visiting
relative from afar would all be exciting starting points for
curriculum planning.

Once you get started, the questions your children ask
will give you plenty of ideas for directions in which to go. To
get a better idea of how this works, go over the example above
and see how many subjects have been included. Think of how
you could include more.

Allow yourself plenty of time to complete a unit. A month would be about the minimum. The maximum will be as long as the interest remains alive. It will vary, so be flexible. Remember, you don't know where it may lead. The planner is only an outline, a guide, a starting point. Looking over the examples above, it is easy to see how the subjects blend together, overlapping and spilling into each other. They are all there just the same. There are probably many subjects that you can not see clearly by looking at the plan. The conversations, lively discussions and debates that you will undoubtedly have over the course of the unit - those concerning moral values, religion, and personal views - are critical elements in a comprehensive curriculum.

Calendar curriculums

Another way to prepare your curriculum is to base it on calendar events. A good reference book available in many libraries is *Chase's Calendar of Annual Events*. It is very lengthy, so be prepared to wade through a lot of information you won't use. However, it is exceptionally thorough, and you are bound to discover events you weren't aware of. It is definitely worth a look if you have the time to invest. If time is at a premium for you, it might be better to buy a *Teacher's Almanac*. We got ours from Educational Insights, 19560 S. Rancho Way, Dominguez Hills, CA. 90220. I've seen similar items in educational stores as well. The one we have is written with school teachers in mind but we've found some fun ideas in it and adapted them to suit us. There are no events during the summer months so we make our own cards for the summer months and we add to the rest as we come across new information. You can take an empty calendar page and fill in the dates. Thomas Edison's birthday could take quite a bit of time to prepare for. You could read books about him, create your own inventions, explore the time in which he lived - the clothing, customs, beliefs etc. and culminate with a grand celebration, inviting your friends for a birthday party at which you present plays, puppet shows, food, costumes or any other products you have from your study. You can take off similarly on any event or anniversary you choose. To see how we geared our curriculum around a calendar, see the planner example from September and October of 1988. By the way, Thomas Edison was homeschooled.

PART 2

The Curriculum Planner

CHAPTER 5

Organization

In a superthick, three-ring binder, insert folders or dividers for each month. Folders work well because the pockets hold items that can't be punched. Between each of the folders leave several blank sheets of paper for journaling and some suitable sheets to mount photos and captions.

In the front of the book, you can put your hours per day (an estimation of approximately how much time you spend on education) and attendance records, general notes for the year and whatever legal requirements you need to include. It is helpful to have a separate page for each student listing the general objectives for the year. Next list the things you want done daily. These may include basics such as personal hygiene, cleaning bedrooms and chores around home, and academics such as reading, writing, religious studies, music and math.

Then divide up the week to cover the rest of their goals and plans. For example, Mondays: reading magazines (setting aside a day for this helps prevent unread magazines from piling up), Tuesdays: cooking and science projects, Wednesdays: social studies and health, Thursdays: history and art, Fridays: movies and games. One game we enjoyed playing was the research game. Each child chooses a topic to look up and report on. This could be as simple as telling what they discovered or doing a more involved project that takes the rest of the day or even into next week. All our board games are educational in nature.

The curriculum planner changes very much from year to year as you try new approaches and drop less effective methods. If you do not like dividing up your week like this, then try something else. Always be open to change and growth. Plan to reevaluate your needs and directions again some time around mid-winter. After a bit of a break, it helps you to get back in gear. This doesn't have to be anything extravagant, perhaps just a re-assessment of your plans.

Look over your subjects for the year and spread them out over the months. Guess at how much time you will need to cover them. Some you'll just touch on, some will take months or years! There is no sure way to know in the beginning, but for the sake of order and organization, try to make projections.

A well thought out curriculum includes objectives, course content, resources, materials and a program evaluation. This is beneficial to have if the laws in your area are especially strict. It's mostly a matter of being well prepared and learning to use terms authorities are most familiar with. Here are my explanations of a few of these often heard terms.

OBJECTIVES and COURSE CONTENT: Clearly describe knowledge, understanding and/or skills you expect the student to learn and how you intend to go about reaching each goal. What specifically will the student do to learn what he/she has set out to learn? Put this on the front of the folder for each month.

RESOURCES: List which books and informational materials you will use and where you will find them. This is an important part of your personal curriculum plan; it is best to plan ahead. Some books may need to be obtained through inter-library loans which take time and forethought. It is worthwhile to have a list of what or whom you plan to use and where they're to be found so when you're ready, you'll know in an instant where to look. As you gather your materials together you will undoubtedly discover some you didn't have listed. Add them as you discover them so you have documentation of what you have used.

MATERIALS: On each month's folder, keep a list of all the materials you will need to gather for planned projects - things like batteries, magnets, wires, nails, glue, paper, anything you might not be able to find in an instant. Begin gathering ahead of time. It is pretty frustrating to get involved in a project only to find you're missing some essential materials and have to order them. Keep a list of resources and

materials in your planner with your objectives page. Check lists a month ahead to allow time to gather everything.

PROGRAM EVALUATION: Evaluations can be in the form of a journal, test results or student products. It is helpful to include written evaluations by the student as well. Short notes written by both you and the student will be very helpful in reviewing what you did, what worked and what didn't. Businesses often provide evaluations for employees to let them know they are appreciated or at least noticed. The evaluations should be mostly positive. Where improvement is needed it should be stated in a constructive manner. The first time we did evaluations, my students thought their evaluations would be much worse than they were. I realized that they hear corrections, coaxing and reminding on a daily basis; I thought I was usually encouraging and positive with them. This was a sign to watch more closely to insure that I communicate effectively. It might be worthwhile to evaluate after individual projects (evaluating the project as well as the student's progress) and to give a more thorough evaluation quarterly or at the semester. Have the students evaluate their own work/effort as well as yours. Then you can evaluate yourself and your students. Again, this doesn't have to be a major undertaking; just a short note will do the job. Of course, if you have more to say at any given time, go for it! [Evaluations can be kept in the family planner or in the student's individual planner.] For some, keeping track of what work was completed and how it went may be as simple as checking off the items on the objectives list as they are completed and perhaps judging them on a scale from one to ten, or even just yes or no, great or yuck! These can be elaborated on as time permits.

FOLDER POCKETS: In here you can keep theater programs, support group newsletters, papers you collected from your students, maps, pamphlets, charts, test materials, etc.

JOURNAL PAGES: These are an indispensable part of your curriculum planner. They are observations and evaluations all in one. They are an excellent way to keep track of all those intangible activities your students engage in, the ones that may not produce something you can keep and show but are nevertheless valuable. It is a delightful way to keep records, well worth the effort. For some, journaling is a difficult habit to get into. Don't feel bad if you can't do it daily, but try to do it regularly. It is a joy to read these over as the years go by.

PICTURE PAGES; Remember the old adage, "a picture is worth a thousand words"? Picture pages give your notebook visual appeal. There are a variety of options for mounting them into your notebook. Check variety stores, stationery stores and photography shops for ideas. It is useful to have captions with these. Take pictures at field trips, pictures of the students working on projects, studying, horsing around, socializing with friends, on trips, everywhere. It really adds an element of authenticity to your book to have your work documented with photos and with the journal.

PERSONAL PLANNERS: Include items such as lists of books read, personal charts and work done, reports, art and support pages. You will probably have many "family subjects" to cover, subjects in which everyone will be involved. These should be kept in the family planner. Individual projects and evaluations pertaining to these subjects can be kept in individual notebooks. We use separate spiral notebooks for math, sketches, creative writing and book reviews. That way it is all together at the end of the year, and we eliminate loose pages lying around the house. The rest was usually kept in the family book until the boys got older and took on the responsibility of some of their own record keeping. Each personal planner should include a copy of general objectives, daily duties and the weekly plans included in the family planner.

CHAPTER 6

Examples

F ollowing are some actual excerpts from my planners over the years. Observe how we completed some plans, replaced others with new ones and scrapped some. THE PLANNER IS MADE TO WORK FOR YOU, NOT THE OTHER WAY AROUND. Stay flexible and open to the moment for your best teaching and learning opportunities.

In 1986 I mainly used World Book's *Typical Course of Study K-12* as a starting point on which to build the curriculum for the year. Inside the folder for August, I found samples of artwork, Kyle's cursive practice and Sean's beginning attempts at writing numbers. Also included was a bit of journaling. September showed fewer examples of work but a bit more journaling.

In 1988 I built the curriculum using an almanac. I changed the format for keeping attendance to a full sized calendar page. In September, again I didn't do as much journaling as I normally like to, but made up for it by including plenty of examples of the work the boys did: math, creative writing, penmanship practice, book reviews, poetry, booklists, awards, and of course, my attendance calendar.

Again in 1992 our planner saw some changes. The boys were older at this point, 14 and 11. I made two separate plans, one for each semester with general goals and plans. The rest we created month by month as we went along. We were much more spontaneous with our planning but more structured in carrying out our plans. More of the documentation for this year was kept by the boys in their own notebooks. Our more organized and structured approach, coupled with the boys being more responsible for documentation, freed up enough time to allow me to take a couple classes at the university this year.

General Plans & Information
1986 - 87

School is 6 hours a day, 5 days a week
Beginning in August

History Day - Thursdays - read 4 history cards
Animal Day - read about any animal
Insect Day - find out about any insect

The boys begin each day with reading.
Kyle reads a chapter aloud from his book.
Sean reads to me and then I read to
him - usually an alphabet book.
Then some work on math and writing.

			Break for snack & activity

I read to them special for the day.
Work on projects

			- Lunch -

Read, science, work on projects or
any extra subjects.

Plans (cont.)

Use dictionary to find the definitions of at least two new words each week.

Make a list of homonyms

Begin cursive – three new letters each week

Write short original stories and poems

Meaning of holidays + some related folk customs

Pet care

Weather Observations

Reading – aloud + silent

Months + Days of Week (poem 30 days hath Sept.)

Use maps + globe in relation to our studies and current events.

    Sean – calendar + clock
    denominations of money
    elementary geometry (shapes)
    personal hygiene
    good eating habits
    Care of teeth
    good clothing habits
    count + write through 99
    count by two.

Books to use (for general plans)

Weather, Breiter

Weather, Kirkpatrick

Just Look at Weather, Rourke

The Four Seasons!, Bright Ideas book

Time! Bright Ideas book

Time and Clocks, Breiter

Holidays of Legend

Holiday Handbooks

   Note: All of the above can be found
   in our personal library

— — — —

For August: Order back issue of
Odyssey magazine or check library
for info on making a solar system
mobile.

August 1986

Star gazing ; see the Perseids and read about them. Try to see Mercury, Venus, Saturn, Mars & Jupiter. Use binoculars and a telescope. Learn about satelites. Motions of the earth.

Count by threes, twos, fives & tens to 100.

Silent reading in increasing amounts & difficulty.

Reading Prose and Poetry aloud.

Begin cursive - abc def ghi jkl

Make a mobile of our solar system.

Books - Space Trip - Bright Ideas book
     Unidentified Flying Objects - Jim Collins
     The Case of the Ancient Astronauts
     Let's Discover Outer Space
     Space - Sievers
All found in our personal library

Kyle ✓
Sean ✓

School Calendar - August '86
✓ = present at least 6 hrs.

Monday	Tuesday	Wednesday	Thursday	Friday
4 ✓	5 ✓	6 ✓	7 ✓	8 ✓
11 ✓	12 ✓	13 ✓	14 ✓	15 ✓
18	19	20 ✓	21 ✓	22 ✓
25 ✓	26 ✓	27 ✓	28 ✓	29 ✓

Materials for September
bead, nail, card, wood, glue, wire
(for weather station)

We talked about ancestry and studied our
own family tree
- Genes and chromosomes and how they affect
  who you are
- Homonyms - we read a book of homonym
  riddles and started a list of homonyms.
- Started using a dictionary to look up
  words, (Kyle isn't very comfortable with
  this yet) then list & define them - later
  I ask him to verbally spell & define them.
- Read "20,000 Leagues Under The Sea" by
  Jules Verne
- Working with fractions Kyle mixed a
  batch of cookies, doubling the recipe as
  he went along - $3/4 + 3/4$, $1/4 + 1/4$, or what
  is $1/4 + 1/2$??
- Spent time in the Public Library
- Read from Odyssey, went star gazing, saw
  the moons of jupiter & our own moon with
  craters & saw mars (all through a telescope)
  Read about the shuttle disaster & it's causes.
  Worked on entries for Odyssey's cover contest.
- Sean worked with cuisinaire rods.
- Began study in watercolor - mixed colors
  - learned proper care of brushes.

September 1986

Community helpers
Transportation - today & yesterday
Common birds, trees & flowers
Forest plants
Life cycle of animals
Begin work with fractions
Count by 3
mno pqr stu vwx y + z in cursive
Weather - build a weather station
  keep track of weather with graphs
  and charts

Wed. - Xtra reading - World, Odyssey etc.
Thur. - History Day - read 4 history cards
Fri - Animal Day & life cycle books -
  animal series   -   Art

Books;   What People Do   – Let's Discover
Trains and Railroads – Konetzke
The Story of Cars   –   "
Airplanes and Balloons – "
   Getting Around – Bright Idea Book
Land Travel – Let's Discover
Trees – Kirkpatrick
Flowers –   "
Our Tree – Wong, Vessel
Watching Animals Grow Up – Wong, Vessel
Insects & Flowers – (Raintree)
   Seeds and Weeds – Kirkpatrick
– All are found in our personal library

Kyle ✓
Sean ✓   September   1986   ✓ = present 6 hrs.

	2✓	3✓	4✓	5
8✓	9✓	10✓	11✓	12✓
15✓	16✓	17✓	18✓	19✓
22✓	23✓	24✓	25✓	26✓
29✓	30✓			

September 1986 Journal

Kyle started a book about a baseball player, Lou Gehrig. He'll read it aloud to me, a chapter a day. / Began multiplication with cuisenaire rods. / Cooking - we made rice crispy treats - Sean counted 40 marshmellows and 6 cups of rice crispies - Kyle estimated ¼ c. butter and did the cooking & stirring. / Began gathering seeds for seed chart. / Read the sound box "B" book to Sean and he started cutting out pictures of words that start with B for an alphabet book he's making. /

Read World magazine. / Filled in the names of the states on a blank US map. / Read "Seasons" to Sean (a Bright Idea Book) / Worked with rods & math books. / Piano lessons

Read "Time!" and "Time and Clocks" - Sean started learning to tell time on his clock.

Cooking - Sean made pudding & Kyle mixed the cake for puddin pockets (cupcakes with pudding inside)

Our read aloud book (for the family) was "The Gift of the Deer" by Helen Hoover. We finished it and discussed what we liked and didn't like in it and also discussed the style of the author. Kyle especially enjoys nature stories.

We read about porcupines and the boys made a porcupine out of an acorn squash and thorns from the thornapple trees. / We've been reading about weather from several books and Kyle made a weather vane. We read from the history cards about KKK, the underground railroad, the Johnstown flood, and sod houses. We read about puppetry and the boys each made a puppet.

The boys are experimenting with felting - layering carded wool and quilting it between fabric, machine washed + dried and/or worked by hand until it's felted. / Kyle is still working on cursive, Sean on printing - both are reading, silently + aloud, daily. / Kyle made brown rice. / They have been working on entries for Odyssey's cover contest.

Sean wants to know where the atmosphere ends and outer space begins. Our encyclopedias are old but they say the troposphere is 6-7 miles thick. They didn't know about the stratosphere. We'll send the question to Odyssey.

Worked on identifying mushrooms
Started bulbs for forcing. Worked on Math - fractions (both boys)

We went horseback riding with Pat Stern, who is interested in Prairie restoration. She showed us some of the fields she's been working on, identifying which plants were "native", and which were undesirable "aliens". The boys learned some of the benefits of original plants (beauty, protein for animals, hardiness) and got a glimpse of what some of this land may have looked like to the early settlers. Afterwards, a long walk in the woods, with plenty of time to observe forest plants and gather some moss (several varieties) and periwinkle and other small woodland plant species for our forest terrarium.

September 1988

Art - *Discover Art* - through lesson 8

Science - Astronomy - read from Isaac
    Asimov's Library of The Universe

History - 4th - Mayflower left Plymoth
    17th - Constitution was signed (see video)
    3rd - revolutionary war officially ended
    " - first pro-football game
    Time capsule.

Social Studies - 27th Native American day
    Sept 30 + Oct 1st - African Holidays
    read about Africa - tell African
    tales.

Health - Better breakfast month!

Books: "Original People" "Nubes of Southern Africa" National Geographic "The Truth About The Moon" "Lion Outwitted by Hare + Other African Tales" "A Revolutionary Idea (We the People)"	Videos: "Design For Liberty" 9/15 "Wake up to Missouri" 9/22 "Great American Chocolate Story" 9/29 Books - from our home library Videos - ordered through catalog.

Journal for September 1988

We listened to music by Scott Joplin. This is the week of summer olympics so we've already spent a fair amount of time watching them. We read about Seoul & South Korea (where they are being held) and learned about the different lifestyles there. We used "National Geographic", encyclopedias and a book from "Children of the World" series called "South Korea". Sean discussed with me what makes America special to him. Then he learned the state bird, flower & tree, and drew the state flag. We read some folklore & watched news.

More olympics. We saw a special program on the division of North and South Korea. It was very emotional and it really reinforced what we read about yesterday. Sean discussed with me a few famous Americans and what they've done to change our world. He talked about George Washington (his favorite president), Harriet Tubman, Albert Einstein, & Thomas Edison and gave a great explanation of who Martin Luther King Jr. was and what he stood for. He also talked about safety and learned the emergency number. Watched "USA Today" - News.

Watched a program on home births vs. hospital births and discussed the pros and cons of each way. (I had one baby each way) We saw a video of a home birth.

Pizza Month   - October 1988 - Fire prevention week - 8th

Art - Discover Art thru lesson 16, painting, mixing colors, masks, drawing heads, faces, sculpture
    Scarecrow

~~Science~~ - The human body - pulse rates, sense of touch,
+ Health } taste and smell, fingerprints, hormones,
    heart, blood, digesting, breathing, bones, muscles.

History - Chicago fire (8th)
        Mahatma Gandhi's birthday (2nd)
        Norway's Leif Erickson Day (9th)
        Camille Saint Saens Birthday (10th) - music!
        Oscar Wilde's Birthday (16th)
        Alaska is officially ours (18th) - see video
        John Adams' birthday (19th)
        Dylan Thomas' birthday (27th)
        Theodore Roosevelt's birthday (27th)
        Columbus Day (10th)
        War of the Worlds

Social Studies - begin study of China
        Chinese holiday (10th) Chinese Kite flying festival
        (8th) - see filmstrip
        Nigeria Independance Day (1st)
        Malagasy Republic Holiday (14th)
        National Heroes Day - Jamaica (20th)
        United Nations Day (24th)

Language Arts - poetry day - 15th

Books: Discover Art 4
Science Project Book of the Human Body
Science in Action: The Living World
Presidents Books
"A Child's Christmas in Wales" by Dylan Thomas
* "The Happy Prince" by Oscar Wilde
* "The Raven" by Poe
* Music by french pianist Camille Saint Saens
"Step into China"
"China" (my country series)
"Look What We've Brought You From Vietnam"
"Living in Hong Kong"
"South Korea" (children of the World)
"Ask about the Human Body"
"Tikki Tikki Tembo"
"Exploring the 50 State"

Videos: "War of the Worlds" (from Melissa)
      "7 Chinese Festivals" 10-6-88
      "The Pipeline"   } 10/13/88
      "A pipeline + Animals" }
      "Recycling - A Way of Life" 10-20-88

* denotes library books - all other books
found in our personal library.

October '88 Journal

Kyle is moving along at a good pace in his 6th grade math book - getting 100% correct most of the time - I'm really pleased with his progress and effort. His handwriting is improving daily, he puts forth good effort there too. He's zipping along in spelling, feeling more encouraged this year and doing a beautiful job in his spelling notebook. In reading, he's determined to finish the entire "Childhood of Famous Americans" series - he's moving right along - reading 1-3 chapters a day. His understanding & retention of the material are excellent - he is a very good reader! He still has a problem with getting down to work early & sticking with it till he's done.

Sean is doing very well in math. He's finished so fast and does more later for fun. His printing is beautiful and he writes lovely poems & letters to people. His reading is improving daily and he's reading with a lot more expression, tackling bigger words and longer books. Good job!! He's having a bit of trouble with spelling so we'll back track on that and try writing (kinesthetic) the words as well as verbal reading & spelling. He shows good interest in other subjects - esp. Science.

General Plans - 1991-1992

Sean - Daily
    Write ½ page in journal
    Read for ½ - 1 hour
    1 math lesson
    music   - clean your room
Monday & Wednesday
        - map work - this month - maps of
natural resources in U.S.
Tues. & Thurs.
        - Work on anatomy or other science
              History

Kyle - daily
    Write in journal   Clean your room
    Read   Music
    Math   French
Monday & Wednesday
    Citizenship in the Community
    World geography - study maps - TAKE OFF!
Tues. & Thurs.
        Anatomy, Biology

Goals for January '92
Read aloud together every evening
Keep Kyle get his merit badges done.
Encourage Sean to read & write more.
Stay organized and focused
Find out about arts grant
Work on budget with Jim
Begin my study on trees in sketchbook
Take good care of myself.

Library Books

Iola Library
Iola pamphlet   – Paintings in the Musée d'Orsay
3 adventure books   – Paintings in the Hermitage
Benjamin Franklin   – Paintings in the Louvre
Franklin
A photo album of the past
Waupaca Library
  Larry Bird - Drive   – Basketball Video
  Kareem   – Indians' Book
Basketball Winning Strategy & Tactics
Touch Typewriting
Create Your Own Career Opportunities
John Pike Paints Watercolors

1-12-92

    Our homeschooling this year is the best yet. We are somewhat more structured, that is, we have a clear goal of what we want to accomplish on a daily basis and we've really been staying with it. We've settled with a method that's very comfortable for all of us. First, I wrote my convictions in a book so I can refer to them, or the boys can, if we forget why we're doing this. That helped a lot. Then we made up monthly charts to keep track of our progress. I expect reading, writing or grammar, math, clean bedrooms and help around the house everyday from both boys. Kyle has a goal to finish his Eagle requirements this month so he has to do merit badge work each day. Each subject equals 1 pt. - Kyle needs 9 pts. each day - Sean needs 7. A job list is posted on the fridge and updated as necessary. Each job is worth a 1 2 or 3 and it takes 6 on the job list to fulfill 1 job point on the chart. This is a wonderful part of our system because I don't like to be responsible for harassing people into helping out. The responsibility is theirs - what needs doing is plainly written so they choose what they feel up to and start working, in their own time, at their own pace. It turns out I've been doing most of the cooking + dishes, Kyle's been sweeping and cleaning the house, Sean's been feeding the squirrel, rabbit + birds, helping cook, unloading the dishwasher and asst. other small jobs. Some of the subjects on the charts for them to choose from to fulfill the necessary points are art, music, current events, cooking, anatomy, shop, social studies, science and health. It's possible for them to finish before noon if they're determined to. Sean tends to drag a bit more than Kyle but keeps up pretty well. Sometimes he needs me to "take him by the hand" so to speak + move him along - esp. after a long break such as Christmas - but in a short while he's back in gear + doing fine. Kyle never needs that - he knows how to apply himself and move through the task at hand. I think they both feel better about themselves and their progress this year. Sean is reading "The Hobbit" and he's really enjoying that. He is working in his anatomy book too - that's going well - we just got some new books from mom on anatomy - I think when Sean finishes his coloring book, we'll read it together + then I'll have him move through this new series. They have beautiful pictures and some fun projects. He is working on grammar, right now learning prepositional phrases, subjects and verbs. He seems to be understanding it pretty well. His math (Saxon) is going well. He's having a hard time keeping his room clean. He bought a pet rat the other day with some money he'd saved. He bought an aquarium & water bottle for it too but the only time it's in it is at night. All day the little fellow sits on Sean's shoulder. Sean named him midnight because he's black/gray. Kyle is reading an adventure called "Boundary Waters". He is being challenged by his math - esp. dividing fractions, but he's a good sport and keeps plodding along... with some help occasionally. He puts in a good effort. I'm continually stressing how thankful he'll be that he's developed a strong math background. His grammar is a breeze for him so far and he also has an anatomy coloring book, though it is much more advanced than the one Sean is using. He has no problem keeping his room clean. He's pushing right along with his merit badge work - a lot of writing & research in many different subjects. He's got quite a bit in communications, citizenship and social studies & he's working on English, Math & Science. He is dependable, responsible, good natured & good humored.

We've all been reading together evenings — John Steinbeck's "The Red Pony" is where we started. I'm not sure what's next. I'll have to snoop around. Jim & I are reading Ben Franklin's Autobiography and other writings of his - he was a remarkable man! Very interesting reading. I picked up 3 very large volumes on art at the library - very old art - we've spent a lot of time looking these over - really shines a light on what people were like long ago - strange! It's been funny & fun - so much so, that I had to ask Jim (kiddingly) if he really thinks it's fair for us to count that time for school... I mean, it was so much fun! We were laughing hysterically! Rolling around & laughing tears!

When the boys have completed their charts for the day they are free to play nintendo, play with friends, go skiing etc.. If they complete the week, then they can have sleepovers with friends. These incentives have been working for us though they may be changed, with time. We've all been accomplishing more & feeling better - the boys argue & fight a lot less now as well. It is clear now that for us the answer was to organize & keep a clear visual reminder of what was expected - with some incentive.

CHAPTER 7

Additional Planner Sections

On Interests, Inclinations, Personalities, Possibilities

It is beneficial to reserve a section for occasional observations on your students' interests, personalities and possibilities (separate sheets for each student). Use it as a place to write things about their personalities and their experiences, much as you would for a resume, that might help them choose a career. This can be a helpful thing to have as they grow up. After a time, the common threads in their lives become very clear. It is not necessary to add to these very often. I keep moving the same page into a new notebook each year, but I am amazed how my observations of four years ago still relate. I just add some of their more recent life experiences and my newest observations. Here's an example of what was written in 1988. It really shows how different my two boys were then and still are.

"Kyle is very athletic, loves to be outdoors in all kinds of weather, likes to be around people, is competitive, is a leader, loves sports, enjoys shopping, creates incredible things with construx, has a great sense of humor, enjoys a challenge, is interested in astronomy, would love to try scuba diving or just about any new adventure, likes science projects, learns quickly, is fascinated with history - all kinds, and politics, likes to travel and is easy to travel with."

That could have been written back in 1985 just as easily; it's mostly common threads. In 1992 I added:

"Kyle is on a soccer team every summer, wants to be a basketball player and is interested in track. He has wanted to be a pilot since he was three, hopes to get his Eagle Award in Boy Scouts next year, is on his second year of working as a camp counselor at a Cub Scout day camp where he leads the Scouts around the camp from activity to activity, keeping them entertained along the way and ending each day with skits and songs he makes up. He is a good worker and loves making his own money, is independent, responsible and dependable. He planned and built - with the help of a crew he assembled - a solid, sturdy, thirty foot suspension foot bridge across a low section of the Ice Age Trail in Wisconsin, traveled to Colorado with scouts and hiked 12,972 ft. up Engineer Mountain. He is

planning another high adventure trip this year, canoeing and backpacking deep in the Canadian wilderness of Woodland Caribou Park in Ontario. This is bear, moose and caribou country. He still has a great sense of humor and is easy and delightful to be with. At 14 Kyle is living and enjoying a full, creative life. He has been homeschooling since the middle of first grade.

1988 - "Sean is artistic, creative, interested in music, dance and drama, loves animals, is quick to make friends and is loyal to his friends. He is good at math and writing, enjoys being helpful and is interested in cooking. He is very sharing and loving, self confident, loves helping people feel better, giving massages, lots of hugs and comforting and encouraging words." Added in 1992: *"Sean thinks he'd like to be a counselor- not, however, a marriage counselor. He is a very philosophical, free spirit. Loves rollerblading, biking, canoeing and swimming, basketball, soccer, roleplaying games and adventure stories. Observed and participated in a college level improvisational dance class, created and sold over a hundred original greeting cards, attended several Sacred Dance seminars, (one time he went alone), where he learned Dances of Universal Peace sang in at least seven different languages and danced dances from many cultures and countries. Here he met and talked with adults and children from all over the area including Chicago, Milwaukee, Minneapolis/St.Paul and places in between. Sean is a confident eleven year old boy living a full, creative life. He has been homeschooling all his life."*

"Observation: Having been segregated in schools into classes according to age, kids become very aware of age differences and "pecking order" or "rank". I notice in Kyle and Sean, the ability to make friends quickly with people of all ages, from adults to children much younger than they. I'm not just talking about getting along here - I mean FRIENDS."

These are two very normal boys who get tired, fight with each other, get bored, angry and sad. They make mistakes just like anyone else. They lie around, eat constantly and need to be told to clean up after themselves. But we try not to focus on those traits. It is essential to focus on the positive aspects of your children.

Read the title for this section again and stay with it. It's really a place for your students to shine. Negative or less desirable traits need to be corrected and forgotten. Focus on the good in everyone. Encourage and motivate your children to be their best selves by showing them their worth.

Support pages

When we first started homeschooling, we got very little support from our families. My parents questioned the validity of our decision. The surprising thing was how much it mattered to me that they support and accept my choice. Though they did not cause any real trouble for me, I felt like I was always defending my decision and more than once I cried as I left their house after visiting. It can be hard and lonely. My husband, on these occasions, kept reminding me that faith and time was all we had, time would tell and in time, they would all see the truth of the matter. Fortunately, this is the case today. Acceptance came about gradually. This became apparent as my mom began to supply us with a large collection of beneficial books. She told me she was proud of me for having the strength to stand up against the world (we didn't know any homeschoolers at the time) for something I believed in. I appreciated that support. Over the years the boys began to speak for themselves. They are unique and wonderful people - interested in and excited about the world they live in. They are well adjusted socially and active in their community. They are dependable, trustworthy, competent and confident. More than once people who have met them were inspired to homeschool their children.

We need to create our own support network for whatever it is we decide to take on. That may be parenting or homeschooling in general or, to be more specific, aviation, dance, music, art, reading, writing - virtually any pursuit. There are many ways to do this. One way is to surround yourself with people who are interested in the same things. Get acquainted with folks who are already doing what you want to learn. Join clubs or organizations and support groups. Sometimes it's not that easy. In some cases you may be the one to start the support group or club. There may not be anyone in your area doing what you love - you will have to educate yourself and then share your knowledge. Subscribe to helpful magazines and read in your area of interest. Cover your personal journal pages or even your walls with pictures and encouraging words, words of wisdom, etc., pertaining to your interest. This will be supportive and encouraging. Learn to be your own best friend, positive and enthusiastic about your endeavors.

In the curriculum notebook, keep a section for home-schooling and self educational support; quotes, book reviews, pictures and articles you've found that support your cause. In their individual notebooks, students can create their own support section. This may spill over onto bulletin boards doors and walls.

I usually keep a few inspirational pieces on my refrigerator door where I will see them regularly. Here is one I wrote to help keep things in proper perspective, for myself and all my visitors: "Welcome to our home. It may be unconventional, chaotic, messy and unorganized but it is vitally alive and generally loving, happy and creative." Don't sit around and expect the world to bring support to you. Actively seek it and draw it into your life. Create your own support systems.

PART 3
Additional Helps

CHAPTER 8

Subject Areas

There are some excellent resource books available to help you decide which books and materials to use. I have used Mary Pride's *Big Book of Home Learning* and Donn Reed's *The Home School Source Book* and I've found them both to be entertaining and very informative. Select topics and approaches in sync with your child's age, ability, level of understanding and attention span. The approach for any given topic will be vastly different for a high school student than for a primary student. Allow for individual levels of interest and understanding. Following are a few ideas to help get you started.

Language Arts

The most important element for a strong foundation in language arts is a READ ALOUD time. This can and should be a family event. Designate a time for this. You can take turns reading. Read from many different styles and cultures. Ideas for good books to read aloud can be found in the library (ask the librarian for suggestions), in Jim Trelease's *Read Aloud Handbook*, and in many of the widely available

catalogs listed in the appendix. Or ask people you know: friends, acquaintances, co-workers and other homeschoolers. Then gather around the fire and READ!!

Books can open up whole new worlds of experience for children. Reading a variety of books will give everyone a background of many different writing styles and techniques as well as a growing vocabulary. Everyone should have an endless supply of reading materials and keep a log with comments on books they've read.

Once you have that basic foundation from which to work, you will discover how closely intertwined reading, spelling and writing are. You can find various methods for teaching these subjects. Use whatever works best for you. Try to include approaches from several learning methods, i.e., songs, plastic magnetic letters, build-a-word games, typewriters, chalkboards and word processors. You may find workbooks that are especially helpful in beginning spelling etc. I have looked for a good writing program but have found that for us the best method is to use some basic books on writing, a good dictionary and lots of practice.

A journal is a popular approach, but for some it is hard to decide where to start or what to write about. Sit down together and brainstorm a list of ideas. Give everyone their own copy. They are sure to find at least one thing on it they feel like writing about. If they have a hard time deciding, write the ideas on slips of paper, to be drawn when needed.

Once in a while, choose a piece of writing to edit and polish. Everyone can help. It is best done as a family project. The writer gets lots of feedback and different points of view. If your family is too small to do this, ask a neighbor or friend to help. Keep the final copy, or perhaps send it in to a contest. It might end up a lucrative endeavor.

For a strong foundation in grammar, we're using *Easy Grammar* by Wanda C. Phillips (available from Timberdoodle). I have the teachers edition which I find very helpful and the boys each move through it at their own pace; my older son is whipping through it at a pretty good speed while my younger son moves through it at a much slower and more methodical rate. It is very thorough and the boys are having no problem understanding it. It covers everything from prepositions and pronouns to punctuation, capitalization, types of sentences and business letters. I like the fact that it wasn't written for any particular grade level but instead is for all ages. The information is in a workbook format (which the boys love), available for anyone at whatever point they want it or feel ready for it.

Science

Science, along with math, is a subject that seems to intimidate a lot of parents. Actually there is so much science in our everyday lives that we hardly even recognize it. The care of houseplants, for example, or starting seeds for the garden, growing sprouts for salads and stir fries, and kitchen herb gardens are all possible starting points for fascinating science

projects. Pet care, aquarium maintenance, feeding and watching birds or studying and logging weather patterns are all
readily available possibilities in many households.

Observe your students. What are their interests? Do
they love working with animals? It may be possible to volunteer at your local humane society or at a pet store. Start bird
study with feeders you make together. Learn to identify their
songs with the help of an audio tape. Use a good bird identification book and a pair of binoculars to observe birds and
keep a journal of your observations. It may be possible to get
involved in wild animal rehabilitation. Check with your

nearest nature preserve to see what kind of programs they have. Farm animals present an abundance of scientific challenges. Depending on your interest, you can take any study as far as you want. Incubate eggs for raising your own poultry. Dairy animals provide endless possibilities from health care and daily grooming to the miracle of birth and caring for the young. The extra milk can be made into cheese, butter, yogurt and ice cream. How does that happen?

Perhaps your students are not interested in animals. Most children, at some point or another, will be intrigued by chemistry and its many mysteries. *Science Experiments You Can Eat* is only one of many simple books available for budding chemists. Older students might want to purchase their own chemistry sets or buy them bit by bit as Edison did. Don't overlook your local high school, university or vocational college as possible resources for information and materials.

Star gazing opens up the door to another galaxy of science possibilities. *Odyssey Magazine* is very readable and understandable. Read it together and spend your evenings out under the stars identifying constellations, stars and planets. Trips to your local planetarium will take on new meaning with your newly acquired knowledge.

The study of anatomy is made more interesting with anatomy coloring books and a model of the human body. Weather study comes alive when you build your own weather station to record rainfall, temperature, wind direction and barometric pressure. More ideas from our experiences include the study of dinosaurs, magnets and electricity, oceans, light and color, solar power, geology, recycling, earthworms, air pressure, pond life and physics. We have worked with all kinds of animals, birds and fishes. Presently we're studying SCUBA for certification so we can observe ocean life up close. (As a related topic, we'll be learning sign language so we can communicate with each under water.)

Environmental education is one science you will probably want to include in your curriculum at some time. It is an important subject for our times. If you want your students to care about the environment then you should care about it. If you want them to do something about it, take some positive steps yourself. There are plenty of opportunities for you as a family to get involved environmentally. You can begin right in your home by learning about the environmental impact of different kinds of packaging, aerosols, hazardous products, animal testing, recycling and composting. Talk to friends about what you do. Eat less meat, buy organic produce, become environmentally conscious. Subscribe to an environmental magazine and plan your curriculum around that. Adopt a cause and put your money, time and/or effort into that. Become involved. Create educational posters and other media to educate the public; give speeches, workshops and presentations on it. (This incorporates speech, community service, English, math/chart making, science, social studies and virtually any other subject you care to include.) You can work in your own community to clean up roadsides and streams or get involved in state or national organizations.

Art Education

Art is dynamic creative expression. The best way to approach art is to dive in. Go to art shows together and talk about the pieces. Get books and videos from the library. Feature different artists from time to time and take the opportunity to look at books and prints of their work and dabble in their techniques. A few times we have paid a fee to sit in the studios of various artists in order to really absorb the process and atmosphere.

Keep creativity flowing and alive; live artfully. Have materials available for experimentation and encourage exploration. As long as your child is actively engaged in creating, leave him/her alone. Just supply the necessary materials and inspiration, back off and let it happen. There comes a time, however, when more help may be sought or needed. Read *Drawing On The Right Side Of The Brain*, *Drawing With Children*, *The Key To Drawing* or any other interesting and helpful books you come across.

Experiment with various sources for inspiration: nature, imagination, decoration, sky lines, buildings, books and magazines, people, music, emotions, experiences, dreams, current events or whatever topic you are studying at the time. Keep a sketch book of ideas, sketches and journaling. Create two and three dimensional art in a variety of mediums, experimenting with various tools and processes. Learn to appreciate beauty in many different forms, natural and man made. Learn about art in everyday life. Discover the variety

of art forms people have created to enhance their lives. Study about opportunities in art. Meet or read about people who make a living in art.

Learn to appreciate and understand art. Observe and discuss the works of various artists. What does art tell us about different people, customs, countries and times? What does our art tell us about ourselves? How can we bring our art out into the world? Some ideas are: sidewalks, murals, art shows, libraries, galleries, clothing, landscaping, props for drama/community theater, greeting cards, stationery, artists markets, posters and banners. Can you come up with more?

Ideas for starting points in art:

Study colors and color families
Investigate the color wheel
Mix colors in paint, pencil, crayon and pastel
Create patterns
Try printmaking
Draw people, stilllife, animals, cartoons
Paint using watercolor, oil, acrylic, tempera
Make collages with fabric, paper or found objects
Sculpt people, animals, pottery or abstract designs
Try some fiber Arts - weaving, stitchery, macrame, quilting, basketry
Work with clay
Make masks

Learn about architecture - forms and shapes in
  buildings
Study color and light - night pictures
Work with stencils
Learn new brushstrokes and techniques for painting
Experiment with drawing different views,
  perspectives, landscapes, crowds of people, cities
Learn graphic design
Discover puppetry

Social Studies

Social studies includes the studies of culture, geography, history, community, citizenship and human rights. In
kindergarten and the early grades the focus is usually on things
familiar and close - family, neighborhood, social living and
local communities. In the middle grades students typically
study the state they live in, American heritage, culture and the
United States. In junior high, global studies, social sciences,
citizenship and history are added. In high school students
often tackle more advanced studies in geography, government, history, economics, psychology and sociology. The
topics you study will fit into many subject categories.

A memorable project to tackle for geography is to
make a paper mache globe. Kits are available for this from
Educational Insights (see appendix for address), or be adven-
turous and go it alone. If you are not ambitious enough for a
project that challenging, get some blank maps to fill in or *The
Geography Coloring Book* by Wynn Kapit. *National*

Geographic magazines are often available for free from sub-scribers after they've finished with them. What a wonderful way to recycle! Subscriptions for *National Geographic* are very reasonable and a worthwhile investment. The magazines provide a wonderful blend of culture, history and geography.

It's a good idea to study citizenship at some point in your homeschooling years. Boy Scouts have wonderful little (merit badge) booklets on citizenship in the community, the nation and the world. Learn about the U.S. Constitution, the Bill of Rights, politics, laws and democracy and other forms of government.

There are plenty of good games to enhance your social studies curriculum. *Take Off!* has a laminated world map for a playing board and airplanes for playing pieces. Playing this game is a fun way to learn the names and locations of all the countries and their capitols and to identify their flags. *Know The U.S.A.* is a trivia game with two levels so young players can play a pretty fair game with their older siblings. National Geographic's *On Assignment* allows for different levels as well. Players travel the world and try to figure out where they are through a series of clues and pictures. *Geosafari* is a self contained computer guessing game that looks like a lot of fun. It may be helpful to share materials (and the expense) with another homeschool family.Before investing in too many games and gizmos, observe your students and try to under-stand what will appeal to them. Then have fun shopping, sharing, borrowing and trading.

Math

Math always seems to start out spontaneously, as do so many subjects in homeschool. Gradually, you begin to add workbooks and maybe even textbooks. Math texts we've found helpful include: *Saxon Math* and *Key Curriculum*. To provide the kind of continuity that is so helpful in the study of numbers, try to make it a regular practice in your home-school to get at least one page of mathematics done each day. This kind of discipline is helpful but, in itself, is not enough. Make mathematics realistic and meaningful by providing opportunities for your students to employ their skills in real life situations as often as possible. When traveling, it can be fun and challenging to have the students do the map reading,

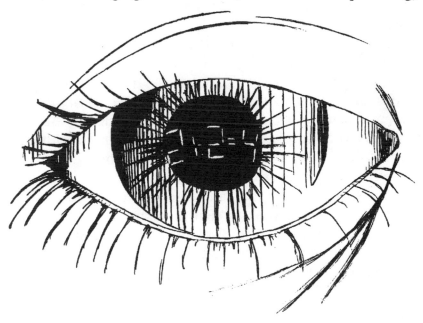

figure the best route, how many miles there are to go, gas mileage and total cost of the trip. Grocery shopping provides various levels of math difficulties from clipping coupons to comparison shopping, figuring price per ounce, weighing produce and computing the cost. At home use budgeting, balancing the checkbook, cooking, statistics, graphs and charts, volumes, density, nutritional information, measurements, weights, money, time and mail order shopping. Keep your eyes open for possibilities; soon you will have more than you can keep up with. It is mostly a matter of allowing for opportunities and taking the time and effort to give the students a chance to do the necessary mental calculations. I am always fascinated at the different approaches we all take to arrive at the same point. We like to compare methods and explore new ways to solve the same problems.

Miscellany

Foreign languages can be learned from tapes, records, books and videos, too numerous to list. *The Learnables* is a fun program, especially for younger students. As you progress, your language studies can be enhanced with well known fairy tales and stories in foreign languages. Word games, such as scrabble or picture bingo (you can create your own) can be played in the language you're studying, or, if you're very new at your foreign language study, then just allow extra bonus points for foreign words. Consider signing as a language to learn. There are books and videos available from your library, or check into taking a class at your local community college.

Basic typing manuals are available in book stores everywhere and are easy to learn from. All you need is a typewriter or computer keyboard and an interest. This subject lends itself quite well to independent learning.

Music education is available to everyone. Start with the library, checking out tapes, records and C.D.s by a variety of artists. Read up on your favorites. Check your local paper for concerts in your area. If there is a university nearby you will probably find numerous free recitals to attend. Musical instruments are available for rent in many music stores and the people there may be able to help you find instructors. Simpler instruments such as pennywhistles, recorders and

harmonicas can be purchased with an instruction book and audio tape to help get you started. *The Lester Family* has tapes and books available that teach singing in two, three and four part harmony and singing in rounds. It is available from *John Holt Book Store. Keyboard Capers* teaches music theory, sight reading and ear training with activities and games. It is available from *The Elijah Company.*

Health is a subject that is very often covered in living day to day. Do you discuss balanced diet and good eating habits? Do you include any activities in your daily routine for fitness? Do you teach your children proper personal hygiene? All of these are health related. Is there more you can do to improve on that? Perhaps there is something in the health field you would like to learn more about: a new way of eating or a different type of exercise or stress management. Expand your horizons. Don't forget about the importance of physical affection for your over-all well being, and be sure to include plenty of kisses, hugs and back rubs in your day.

CHAPTER 9
On High School

High school seems to be a time when many home-schoolers begin to doubt their ability to provide an adequate education. Home-schooling is not synonymous with isolation. Remember, you don't have to do it all alone. The world is your classroom. You have taken the liberty to design your own education and in so doing, you have more freedom to choose what teachers you want, your actual learning environment and what approach you want to take. Opportunities abound, outside the home setting, to expand on or enhance one's education. You might be able to set up a work-study program where the student spends part of his/her day at the job site or in a studio or office participating in meaningful work and really getting a feel for the trade.

One common concern is the lack of equipment in most homes such as computers or lab equipment. There are a wide variety of options if you're open to explore them. It may be possible to work out an agreement with the schools to use the equipment evenings or weekends, or check into the possibility of taking one or two classes at the high school. Some home-schooled high school students take adult night school classes. Public libraries have learning media available. Universities are an option as well. Look in as many directions as you can: apprenticeships, work/study, private tutors etc.

Some fear the lack of an accredited high school diploma may cause future problems career-wise or in college entrance. Job applications usually ask how many years you have completed in school. Sometimes they ask for the name of the school you graduated from. It is a simple matter to give your school a name. Some homeschooling families present their graduates with a diploma. For college entrance you will want to back this up by keeping accurate records of everything studied in high school and all accomplishments to present. Be sure to include results and information on any classes taken as well as listing lectures attended, job experience or anything that might be of interest. Homeschoolers are subject to the same entrance exams as anyone else. It might be a good idea to pick up a book on SATs or other standard achievement tests and study them before taking them. The time spent preparing for the tests will count towards a high school credit in general education or wherever you care to fit it in. When applying to the college of your choice, homeschooling can be an asset. It sets you apart from the crowd. You may have something really unique to add to the school. There are several good books that address the issue of college after homeschool. Some are listed in the appendix at the back of this book. There are numerous benefits to homeschooling through high school. There is literally a world of subjects to choose from. You are not limited to the classes offered by your local school. You can continue to create your own program tailored to your personal interests. About half the credits earned by high school students are electives. Check your local high school to see what is offered. Most if not all of what is being offered there can easily be added to a home program. There is a vast array of educational materials available today.

It is wise to include some of the customary electives in your program, such as foreign languages, music and business courses. These establish the well rounded curriculum that colleges and businesses are looking for. There is still plenty of room to fill in with elective credit courses which you create. Many homeschoolers come up with intriguing and imaginative courses that have never been offered for high school credit before. You have a world of options open to you.

High school credits are measured in time. 180 hours of study equals one credit or 90 hours per semester. The graduation requirements at our local high school are as follows:

> Four (4) credits of English
> Two (2) credits of Mathematics
> Two (2) credits in Science
> One (1) credit in U.S. History
> Two (2) credits in Social Studies
> Seven semesters of Physical Education or 1.5 credits
> One-half (.5) credit of Health
> One-half (.5) credit of Computer Studies
> A passing grade in the classroom phase of Driver Education

In addition to the required courses nine (9) credits are required for a total of twenty-two and one-half (22.5) credits. The Board of Education encourages students to enroll in courses to earn credits in vocational education, foreign languages, the fine arts and all areas.

You can check your local high school's curriculum to see how they cover these subjects, or you can create your own plan. It is best to diversify.

ENGLISH includes writing, grammar, literature, vocabulary, spelling and speech.

MATH can be business math, consumer math, computers, algebra, geometry, trigonometry and calculus.

SCIENCE can cover environmental education, biology, chemistry, physics, aerospace, astronomy, electricity, electronics, food science, geology, anatomy, physiology.

HISTORY might be world history, American history, local history or even family history. You can use newspaper files, the library, historical novels, people in your community, relatives, museums and family histories.

SOCIAL STUDIES can take you into American government, economics, current events, psychology, sociology or geography- physical and political.

HEALTH and PHYSICAL FITNESS include fitness, wellness, sexuality, growth and development and diet.

ELECTIVES- a good mix might include foreign language, music, art, religion, record keeping, typing, business education, computers and driver's education.

The requirements for record keeping vary from one area to another. We record the number of hours we spend in educationally stimulating pursuits each day, (I realize this is impossible to do, but the way the laws are created, it is beneficial to try and play along) usually at least 6 hours each day. The important thing is to keep complete records of all you accomplish. Do this daily, and don't miss a thing. It will pay off in the end to have this documentation, however you decide to use it. Use several methods for your record keeping: journaling, charts and a simple form on which you jot notes on what you accomplished each day. Once a week, sit down with these notes and rewrite them for a more accurate account of your achievements. We like to have some kind of student product for each "credit" or completed unit of study.

CHAPTER 10

Projects And Products

To finalize a unit of study or credit, have the students create an end product. Not only is this fun and educational, but the students have something tangible to show for all their time and energy. People usually think of written reports as a typical end product. There is no need to limit yourselves to that. Be creative in coming up with ideas for products. Write a play and perform it; make a video; record foreign language stories, recitations, or music you performed. Write about or photograph a meal you prepared; make a game about what you studied or a photo album documenting work you did. This is just a beginning list of possible end products. Use it and add to it. Keep a record of these products if you can't keep all of the products themselves. (The footbridge Kyle built was not ours to keep but we documented it with photos and a story he wrote about the project.)

POSSIBILITIES FOR PROJECTS

animations
fiction
art shows
food
audio tapes
graphs
autobiographies
identification charts
baked foods
interviews
banners
inventions
bibliographies
journals
biographies
photos
books
brochures
building
bulletin boards
board games
cartoons
clothing
collections
community service
computer programs
crossword puzzles
dance
debate

demonstrations
designs
diagrams
dioramas
documentaries
dramas
drawings
editorials
essays
fact files
field trips

Undoubtedly, you will come up with more ideas for projects to suit your individual style and subject.

CHAPTER 11

Atmosphere

You may have noticed how some environments are really conducive to learning and exploring and others feel blocked or dead. Put some thoughtful planning and effort into your surroundings and create a healthy environment for learning.

Attitude

The place to start is inside. How are your attitudes? Are you running up against constant resistance from your children? Does it get to be too much of a power struggle to accomplish anything? Your relationship with your children is your first priority. A child with a healthy self image and a foundation based on love can accomplish anything, but all the education in the world is no help to a person who is miserable inside. So take the time you need to build a healthy, loving relationship with your children. Once that is established, everything will be easier for everyone. The best example is for you to work yourself into the curriculum and keep learning.

Surroundings

It is nice to have an area to study - a place set aside for your desk and supplies. However, we have never had such a place and we get by just fine. Our sofa is the preferred spot for research and reading, the kitchen table for math, art and writing. You will need one central location for materials where you'll keep a supply of writing papers, art paper, scissors, pencils and pens, art supplies, paper punch, tape, glue, rulers, markers, compass, protractors and other assorted odds and ends for study. The time it takes to organize such an area and teach everyone to keep it organized is well invested. It always pays to be organized. Also, make sure you have proper lighting wherever most of the studying is done.

When doing a unit study, highlight it by displaying some of the books you will be using and any other related items of interest. This helps to spark the interest of the students. Often that's all that is needed to get them going. You'll wake up to find them absorbed in books that otherwise would have been collecting dust on your shelves or in the library. As you work your way through a unit study, display art projects and other work the students complete.

How Much Structure?

You have to decide for yourself how much you're able to let go of completely and how much structure you need to be happy and comfortable. For most of us this means a certain amount of structured work. Setting goals, developing a clear focus and working to achieve those goals can be a positive and personally empowering experience. It is an excellent method for developing self-discipline and for getting from one point to another. What is called for is a balance. It is my experience that a comfortable combination of natural, free learning and goal setting and planning works best.

Generally, for younger students, natural learning will be the dominant mode. As the students mature and develop more of an awareness of self, goals, interests, and the world around them, there is more need and desire for a bit of planning. In high school, the scales tip the other way. Students tend to have more goals and a clear set of plans on how to reach them. It is best if the curriculum you develop is a collaborative endeavor. It should be a combination of what you need for your peace of mind, to comply with the law and keep peace in the family, and what the student is interested in learning about. Hopefully, you will all find a beautiful working balance, but be prepared to make adjustments on a daily, weekly and monthly basis.

You might need more structure on certain days and less on others. I let the boys determine that. When they lie around bickering and fighting and they're obviously getting on each others' (or my) nerves, that's a sure cry for some direction and guidance. If, on the other hand, they are completely engrossed in a project, and opportunities are popping up for them to experience that knowledge in greater depth, then that's a sign to lighten up on the structure and take advantage of the enthusiasm and opportunities when they are best. The structure of your days may also be determined by requirements mandated by the Department of Public Instruction or your local school administrators. What you need to do to comply with the law will vary from one area to the next. It is your responsibility to become familiar with the laws concerning home-education in your state and work those requirements into your curriculum. A publication put out by Holt Associates, Inc., *Growing Without Schooling*, prints an annual directory which includes listings of helpful teachers, lawyers, professors, psychologists, school districts, and resource people. Home School Digest, P.O. Box 249, West, Texas 76691, also has helpful directory listings. There is a homeschooling computer board through which you can communicate with homeschoolers all across the country. The resource person for this is Cindy Duckert, 229 Berkley Dr., Neenah, WI. 54956.

Be sure to leave lots of empty time - kids don't need a constant barrage of data and information to keep them thinking or entertained. On the contrary, too much interference cuts off creative thought which needs time to blossom. It is only when free time is not made available that we need to create "special classes" to encourage creative problem solving and creative thinking...another separate class, another fragmented piece of the whole child. The point here is that you should never feel obligated to fill up every hour of every day with some type of stimulation. Don't feel that the "empty space" in your days is necessarily wasted, or that you're doing nothing. If you need to label it, label it "creative processing" or "natural inspiration" or "centering and relaxation," a wellness technique we could all use. You can fit it into whatever category you are most comfortable with...health and wellness, art/music, philosophy...you name it. Go ahead and write it in wherever it makes you happy. Just recognize and appreciate its importance and don't underestimate its value as an intrinsic part of your personal curriculum.

Incentives

Inevitably, you will reach a point, or more likely many points, where a little outside incentive is needed. We all come to these points from time to time when it is difficult to go on with the task at hand. Perhaps we have lost interest or come upon a hurdle without enough energy to overcome it. How do you handle such difficulties? A look at your own methods may help you to assist your students in dealing with the situation when it arrives. Maybe a bit of a break is needed. If I am trying to finish something in an afternoon, I'll often offer myself something like a romantic hot bath at the end of the day, complete with bubbles, a good book, a cup of tea and some of my favorite music. Sometimes that's all it takes to get me through. Encourage your students to find a personal treat they can offer themselves. It's a good idea for them to work on these challenges in their own way. At times, you might want to plan special projects at specified intervals. For example, when we were studying the human body, we made a plan whereby, if we completed our studies by a certain hour each day for a designated length of time, we would buy ourselves a model of the visible man and put it together. For you, it could be a field trip or other special activity or event planned for when you've reached your goal. Work together on this one. You are sure to come up with some truly creative solutions and ideas. Be sure you keep the promises you make to yourself or others as incentives.

We cannot expect all children to automatically develop a strong pattern of self discipline. Look around and you will see that most adults haven't achieved it. Helping your students develop self discipline can be a challenging process- sometimes encouraging, nudging and pushing - other times releasing, trusting, and allowing the space necessary to develop.

Most adults have a built-in incentive to get them through days, projects or jobs they don't enjoy; it's called a paycheck or keeping your job. A lot of kids need these little built in incentives too. My boys ask for it. I have an old letter from one of them stating: "Mom, you have to make me do my work or else I can't play soccer." I never wanted to be in the position of pushing them to do things, but sometimes it's necessary and they want it. At those times we sit down together and write up a plan including what is expected to be done and what the consequences will be for not doing it. This plan has to be revised as our lives and circumstances change, but it works quite well.

It is really helpful to have charts or lists of expectations and goals. Keep them where you can refer to them often. When someone is asking for permission to go to a friend's house or off on some other excursion, together you can make a quick check of the chart to see whether all of their requirements for the day have been met. Charts are a visual aid to help you stay on course. This has been especially helpful to me because I usually have my mind on other things and don't always remember all of our plans quickly.

A Few Ideas For Incentives:

Peanut Butter Day
Trip to the rock shop
Have a cookie party
Pizza party
Home baked bread day
Stargazing sleepover party
Game day
Magazine day
Movie day
Popcorn party
Hat day (get hats for everyone to wear and read *Hats For Sale*)

Helpful Ideas

Each time you return from the library, sit down with all the new books you checked out and on a piece of paper write the title, author and person or persons for whom the book was checked out. At the top of the page, write the date the books were checked out and the due date. This provides you with a handy record to refer to when you're trying to round up all those books. You'll know when the search is up. You'll also have a record of the kinds of books your students were using at any given time. Keep this in your organizer in the proper month. It helps to mark the calendar with the due date, or even a few days earlier so you remember to return them on time.

 For younger students you can prepare a "school" box with new crayons, scissors, glue, workbooks and whatever items you want. Save it until school officially starts in the community when all their friends are getting new clothes, notebooks, pencils and crayons. Kindergarten and early grade school children feel as if they're missing out on something great when they see their peers preparing for this big event. My students are older now, but they still give me a list of what they'll need for the coming year. Pens, pencils, art supplies, a trapper-keeper or folders to keep all their work organized, books and notebooks are the types of items on their lists. They enjoy getting ready for a new year and appreciate getting fresh new supplies. This does not,

however, have to end up being a major investment for you. If you keep the basics on hand - paper, pencils, pens etc. - you can get everything else you need for free. (See Deciding What To Study)

CHAPTER 12

Summer

Acknowledge the educational value of the activities your students engage in during summer. It can help reduce the anxiety sometimes felt during the school year about whether or not you are working hard and fast enough. Hard and fast academics become irrelevant when you've seen your students initiate and follow through on interesting meaningful activities.

For most young people, summers are filled with activities. They can get most of their phy ed during these months swimming, biking, skateboarding, rollerblading, running, boating, jumping, climbing and skipping. It seems like constant motion. However, there will be moments when they actually slow down and run out of ideas. Keep a section in your planner for summer activity ideas. These can be divided for outside and inside or rainy day activities. Be sure to include everyone when brainstorming for ideas. Post the list for the students to check.

Summer activity ideas:

baseball
tubing
soccer
football
frisbee
swimming
camp out
explore with hand lens
explore with binoculars
go to park
go on nature hike
scavenger hunts
bike rides
horseback riding
write a book
visit the zoo
go to the library
make sail boats from scraps and float them in a river
    lake or pool
picnics
cooking
plant something
crafts-keep several craft books on hand w/supplies
drawing and painting
have a party

build a fort
make up games
put on a play or puppet show
draw with chalk on cement
hopscotch
jump rope
bird watching
read a book
catch lightning bugs
fly a kite
try something new
make a list of things you'd like to try or learn about

Travel

To get the most out of traveling plan ahead. Write to chambers of commerce in the places you plan to visit even if you have been there before; you might discover something you were not aware of. Kids think its fun getting the information packets chambers of commerce typically send including brochures on places of interest and maps of the area. If you're interested, you can find books or videos to further your study on the area.

Take turns reading maps or have a designated navigator. Buy a budget planner and together project expenses including food, gas, lodging, tickets, souvenirs etc.. Keep track of gas prices in different locations.

Have each family member keep a journal. These can be written, or they may take the form of sketch books, photo journals or cassette tapes with someone narrating the events of the trip. A scrapbook in which to keep flyers and brochures, ticket stubs, pressed flowers and sketches is fun for younger students. Help them address postcards to themselves and mail them so that when you get home they can assemble the postcards into a book. Be sure they write something about the place on the back of the cards before you mail them.

Take binoculars and a hand lens to study constellations, insects, wildlife and other natural wonders. You might want to bring along bird and insect identification books or coloring books that accurately depict butterflies, seashells, fossils, cactus and other plants and animals...and don't forget the colored pencils! Our favorites are watercolor pencils. They work just like regular colored pencils but a drop of water turns them into beautiful watercolors! Easy to use!

You can get tapes that teach you about the songs of birds, loons, wolves and frogs. Perhaps this would be a good time to learn a foreign language or listen to a recording of a good book read. Remember to include a variety of different types of music tapes: classical, jazz, blues, boogie woogie and sing alongs. Bring something for everyone to enjoy. These are the things of which wonderful memories are made!

Before you go, learn some basic stretching and aerobic exercises to gently awaken and revitalize your cells and refresh you all along the way. Be aware of what you are eating and how it affects your bodies and dispositions. Use this time to foster an awareness of the qualities of different foods and how they help a body function. Note the vitamins or minerals, fat content, fiber, freshness, vitality and general nutritional value of each food eaten. Try to keep snacks healthy.

Writing a curriculum can be a lot of fun. Take your time over the summer and work on it in segments. The time spent planning now is well invested. With all your goals, plans, resources and charts organized and in one easy to find location you will save many valuable hours. Your plan becomes your trusty friend as the year rolls on and you refer to it and realize your goals. Documentation occurs easily as you progress through the years and as time passes you will be amazed at your progress as you look over your planners from past years.

Appendix

There are thousands of books, perhaps millions, for you to choose from. So many, in fact, that I almost hate to list any. It seems so limiting. The resource list in chapter 3 is the best place to begin. I'll list only a few books we've used or found helpful but it's really up to you to find what works and what doesn't. After a while you won't make as many mistakes. It'll be easier to tell, just by looking at a book or item, whether or not it will work with the student for whom it is intended. Be willing to admit it if a book you've acquired isn't reaching your student. With so many materials available it just doesn't make sense to force anyone to use materials that aren't suited to them. (If you purchased a loaf of bread, then discovered it was bad, you wouldn't expect everyone to eat it.) Sometimes we can fix a mistake of this sort by returning for refund or exchange, or by trading with someone else, but sometimes we just have to set it aside and forget it - chalk it up as a mistake and move on.

Catalogs

Educational Insights, 19560 S Rancho Way Dominguez Hills, CA 90220. We bought our globe kit and teacher's almanac here.

Dover Publications, Inc. 31 East Second St., Mineola, NY 11501. Plenty of inexpensive books of all kinds.

Timberdoodle, E 1610 Spencer Lake Road Shelton, WA 98554. Great catalog, competitive prices.

Key Curriculum Press, P.O. Box 1304-S Berkeley, CA 94702. 800-338-7638. Consumable math- the kids love it!

Holt Associates, 2269 Massachusetts Ave., Cambridge, MA 02140. Wonderful catalog.

Family Pastimes, RR4 Perth, Ontario, Canada K7H 3C6. Catalog of cooperative games.

Barnes and Noble, 126 Fifth Ave., New York, NY 10011. Hundreds of books, fabulous sales.

Science News Books, 1719 N St. NW, Washington, DC 20036. Great ideas for science studies. They have a nice little magazine too.

Usborne Books, EDC Publishing, 10302 E. 55th Place, Tulsa, OK 74146. British books with that fun British format in sciences, social studies and how-to. Good info and cross-cultural.

Dale Seymour Publications, P.O.Box 10888, Palo Alto, CA 94303. Books and equipment for math (some really neat mental math), science, language arts, creative thinking, art.

Elijah Co., P.O. Box 12483 Knoxville, TN 37912-0483. 615/691-1310

The Sycamore Tree, Inc., Educational Services, 2179 Meyer Place, Costa Mesa, California 92627

Art

Drawing on The Right Side of The Brain and *Drawing on The Artist Within* by Betty Edwards

Drawing With Children by Mona Brookes

The Key to Drawing by Bert Dodson

The Young Masters Home-Study Tutorial Art Program, Gordon School of Art, 2316 Oakwood Ave, GreenBay, WI 54301. Formal training in the visual arts for children. We never actually enrolled, we may, it looks interesting.

KidsArt, P.O. Box 274, Mount Shasta, CA 96067. Mail art. Pen pals send decorated envelopes and art/letters. For info send your name, address and two 29 cent stamps.

Math

Saxon Math. We got ours from: Sycamore Tree Educational Services, 2179 Meyer Place, Costa Mesa, California 92627.

The Adams Book Co. will sell used text books to individuals. Call first to see if they have the book you want. If they do, find out what the total price is plus shipping and handling charges and mail a check for the complete amount with your order. They don't have a catalog but I know of people who have purchased Saxon Math through them at a substantial savings. The phone number to call is 1-800-221-0909.

Key Curriculum, Math Key Curriculum, Press P.O. Box 2304 Berkely, CA 94702.

Cut and Assemble 3-D Geometrical Shapes by A.G.Smith (Dover).

Language Arts

Writing Down The Bones by Natalie Goldberg

Written and Illustrated By by David Melton

Market Guide For Young Writers by Kathy Henderson

On Writing Well by William Zinsser

Cricket, The Magazine for Children, Carus Corporation, 315 Fifth Street Peru, Illinois 61354

The Read Aloud Handbook by Jim Trelease

Easy Grammar by Wanda C. Phillips (we got ours from Timberdoodle)

The Elements of Style by Strunk Jr. and E.B.White

The Elements of Editing by Arthur Plotnik

The Elements of Grammar by Margaret Shertzer

The Scott, Foresman Handbook For Writers by Maxine Hairston, John J Ruszkiewicz

The Young Writer's Handbook by Susan and
Stephen Tchudi

Science

Cobblestone, Cobblestone Publishing Inc., 20 Grove,
St. Peterborough NH 03458

National Geographic, National Geographic Society,
Washington, DC 20036

Science News Books, 1719 N St. NW, Washington,
DC 20036

Odyssey Magazine, Kalmbach Publishing Co., 21027
Crossroads Circle, Waukesha, WI 53186

WonderScience, American Chemical Society, P.O.
Box 57136, West End Station, Washington, D.C.
20037

Resource Books

Home Learning, Vols. 1-4 - Mary Pride

The Home School Source Book - Donn Reed

World Book Encyclopedia - World Book

Chase's Calendar of Annual Events

John Holt Book Store, Holt Associates, 2269 Massachusetts Ave., Cambridge, MA 02140

Consumer Information Catalog, S. James Consumer Information Center, P.O. Box 100 Pueblo, Colorado 81002

High School and College

Supreme School Supply Co., 625 S. Dettloff Drive, P.O. Box 225, Arcadia, WI 54612. Supply house from which forms for diplomas may be purchased.

The 1993 What Color Is Your Parachute? A practical Manual for Job-Hunters and Career Changers - Richard Bolles

The Whole Work Catalog, Box 297-UE, Boulder CO 80306

College Degrees By Mail - John Bear

The Question Is College - Herbert Kohl

Your Hidden Credentials - Peter Smith

Peterson's SAT Success - Joan Davenport Carris, Michael R Crystal

The Teenage Liberation Handbook: How to Quit School and Get a Real Life Education - Grace Llewellyn

Bear's Guide to Earning Non-Traditional College Degrees - John Bear

College Admissions : A Guide For Homeschoolers - Judy Gelner

Ten SATs - *The College Board.* Actual SATs and suggestions for preparing to take the SAT.

Conquering Test Anxiety: or How To Psyche Up for the SAT, GRE, GMAT, LSAT, MCAT, or any other standardized test - Fiore, Neil and Susan C. Pescar.

Cracking the System: The SAT - Robinson, Adam and John Katzman.

Getting College Course Credits by Examination to Save $$$ - Gene R. Hawes.

Peterson's Independent Study Catalog

Earn College Credit For What You Know - Susan Simosko

Books to help prepare for the GED

The Cambridge Pre-GED Program - New York: Cambridge Book Co.

Passing The GED: A complete Preparation Program for the High School Equivalency Examination - Scott, Foresman. Glenview, IL: Scott, Foresman and Co., 1987.

Testing Companies

College-Level Examination Program (CLEP), DAN-TES, and Advanced Placement Program (APP) are all handled by Educational Testing Service, Princeton, NJ 08541

ACT-Proficiency Examination Program (ACT-PEP), American College Testing Program, P.O. Box 168, Iowa City, IA 52243.

Games

On Assignment - National Geographic Society Travel Game with lots of pictures and information.

Know the USA (Pressman) Trivia-type quiz game.

StarWords - A cooperative word game. We've played in English, Spanish and French.

Our Town - Cooperative real estate and city planning. Players work together to develop a stable economy.

Wff n Proof - Game of logic.

Take Off! - Learn all the countries, their capitols and flags.

Picture Bingo - Make your own with magazine pictures or your own drawings and play in any language.

Scrabble, Chess, Yahtze, Dominoes, Dice - good old fashioned, inexpensive games.

Teaching and Learning

In Their Own Way - Thomas Armstrong

Growing Up Learning - Highlights, Ed. by Walter B. Barbe

Dumbing Us Down: The Invisible Curriculum of Compulsory Schooling - John T. Gatto

Teach Your Own - John Holt

Homespun Schools - Raymond and Dorothy Moore

Homeschool Burnout - Raymond and Dorothy Moore

You Can Teach Your Child Successfully - Ruth Beechick

Home Learning: Vols 1-4 - Mary Pride

Growing Without Schooling - bi-monthly magazine includes articles by students and their parents, many suggestions for activities and resources, very supportive information on how different families approach homeschooling and its challenges.   2269 Massachusetts Ave., Cambridge, MA 02140.

Homeschooling For Excellence - David and Micki Colfax

Relationships

Siblings Without Rivalry - Adele Faber and Elaine Mazlish

How to Really Love Your Child and How to Really Love Your Teenager - Ross Campbell

How to Talk so Your Kids Will Listen and Listen so Your Kids Will Talk - Adele Faber and Elaine Mazlish

Whole Child Whole Parent - Berends

Index

A

B

C

Simplify your curriculum planning with

<u>Curriculum Planners</u>

Looseleaf packets ready to insert in your
3-ring binder, these planners contain all the **forms**,
charts and **instructions** you'll need to plan, organize
and document your curriculum for a whole year.
You'll find all the planner sections you read about in
Write Your Own Curriculum and **MORE!** There are
monthly dividers, **picture pages** and plenty of
space for journalling. There is even an **almanac** to
help you plan your studies around special events.

The family planner is ideal for families with young
students or in a situation where an adult is doing the
planning and documenting.

As your students become more independent they will
each want their own planner. The student planners
encourage organizational skills and foster a sense of
personal responsibility in the student.

With their own planners, students can plan their
course of study for the year and document their own
progress. A valuable addition to any homeschool
program!

For your convenience, there is an order blank on the
back of this page...

Order Form

Telephone orders: (715) 345-1795. Have your Visa or MasterCard ready.

Postal orders: Whole Life Publishing, P.O. Box 936, Stevens Point, WI 54481-0936, USA.

Description	Price	Qty	Total
Write Your Own Curriculum	$12.95		
Family Curriculum Planner	$29.95		
High School Curriculum Planner	$29.95		
Middle Grades Curriculum Planner	$29.95		
Primary Curriculum Planner	$29.95		
Add 5.5% for Wisconsin orders			
Shipping $2.00 1st item, $.75 for each additional item			
Total			

Name: _____

Address: _____

City: _____ State: _____ Zip: _____

Payment:

☐ Check   ☐ Visa   ☐ MasterCard

Card number: _____

Name on card: _____ Exp. Date ___/___

Signature: _____

Call and order now